W9-ARK-864

weird but true!

NEW YORK CITY

NATIONAL
GEOGRAPHIC
KiDS

weird but true!

NEW YORK CITY

300 BIZARRE FACTS ABOUT THE BIG APPLE

NATIONAL GEOGRAPHIC
WASHINGTON, D.C.

Bronx

Manhattan

Queens

Brooklyn

Staten Island

4

All together, the **five boroughs—** Manhattan, Brooklyn, the Bronx, Queens, and Staten Island— that make up New York City are almost the same size as **eight Walt Disney Worlds.**

guten tag

namaste

salam

hola

hello

More than **200 languages** are spoken in New York City.

ciao

aloha

ni hao

bonjour

konichiwa

It is **illegal** to honk your car horn in the city, except to **warn of danger.**

New York City's first gas-powered taxis were red and green.

On a **clear day** you can see six states from the Empire State Building observation decks.

The Empire State Building has its own **ZIP CODE.**

In 2019, four "show globes"—10-foot (3-m)-tall snow globes featuring Broadway shows—were on display in Times Square.

DISNEP
PRESENTS

THE

LION KING

lionking.com

Rafiki wax figure

NO SITTING

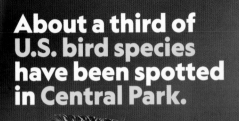

About a third of U.S. bird species have been spotted in Central Park.

In 2016, a man set a record by visiting every New York City subway stop in 21 hours, 28 minutes.

Canal Street Station

Ⓐ Ⓒ Ⓔ

UNTIL THE 1920s,
MAY 1 WAS "MOVING DAY"
IN NEW YORK CITY—
THE ONE DAY OF THE YEAR
WHEN APARTMENT
RENTALS EXPIRED.

The city's **largest public library** building contains **125 miles** (200 km) of bookshelves.

The **library** has a collection of **40,000** historical restaurant **menus.**

More than

100
billionaires
live in New York
City—the most
of any city in the
world.

When
GEORGE WASHINGTON
was named president of
the United States,
New York City—not
Washington, D.C.—was
the **COUNTRY'S CAPITAL.**

A baby is
born in
New York
City every
4 minutes
24 seconds.

If the borough of **Brooklyn** were its own city, it would be the **fourth largest city** in the United States.

NEARLY 400,000 PEOPLE PASS THROUGH TIMES SQUARE EVERY DAY.

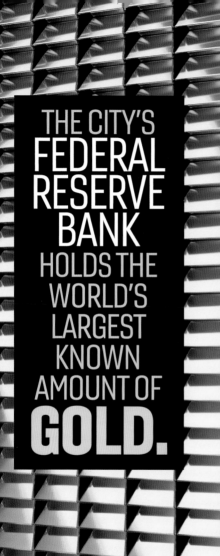

THE CITY'S
FEDERAL RESERVE BANK
HOLDS THE WORLD'S LARGEST KNOWN AMOUNT OF
GOLD.

The gold **vault** houses some

500,000

gold bars,

which together weigh as much as

900

African elephants.

More people live in New York City than in 39 of the 50 states.

THE STATUE OF LIBERTY ARRIVED FROM FRANCE IN 1885 IN 214 CRATES—AND REMAINED UNASSEMBLED FOR ALMOST A YEAR.

That's weird!

When **horses and buggies** were a popular mode of transportation in the city, almost **500 tons** (450 t) of **manure** were collected from the streets every day.

Because of the arched ceilings in Grand Central Terminal, if you whisper into

one corner, a person in the corner across the room can hear you.

THERE HAVE BEEN MORE THAN 13,000 PERFORMANCES OF *THE PHANTOM OF THE OPERA* ON BROADWAY, THE LONGEST RUNNING BROADWAY SHOW.

MORE THAN 500 POUNDS (227 KG) OF DRY ICE ARE USED FOR EACH PERFORMANCE.

The price of a *PIZZA SLICE* and a *SUBWAY RIDE* have been about equal for the past *50 YEARS.*

Endangered species

were projected onto the side of the **Empire State Building** in 2015 to draw attention to the **rare animals.**

FORTY-FOUR NEW YORK CITY SUBWAY CARS WERE DROPPED IN THE OCEAN OFF THE COAST OF MARYLAND, U.S.A., TO CREATE AN ARTIFICIAL REEF.

Nursery rhymes play every half-hour on Central Park's Delacorte Clock and change with the seasons.

IN 1886, THE FIRST **TICKER-TAPE PARADE** IN NEW YORK CITY CELEBRATED THE DEDICATION OF THE **STATUE OF LIBERTY.**

During the New York City Ballet's *Nutcracker* performance, an artificial Christmas tree "grows" from 12 to 41 feet (3.7 to 12.5 m) tall.

New Yorkers drink almost **seven times more coffee** than people in other U.S. cities do, a survey found.

NEW YORK CITY HAS 14 MILES (23 KM) OF PUBLIC BEACHES.

Some **600,000 dogs** live in New York City—that's about the human population of **Baltimore, Maryland, U.S.A.**

The **lost-and-found** department at **Grand Central Terminal** recovers about **30,000 items** a year from the **city's trains.**

More than half the items are **returned** to their **owners.**

The **Eloise Suite** at the Plaza hotel looks like the **illustrations** from the Eloise children's books.

The **portrait of Eloise** that hangs in the Plaza's Palm Court is a replacement—the original was **stolen and never found.**

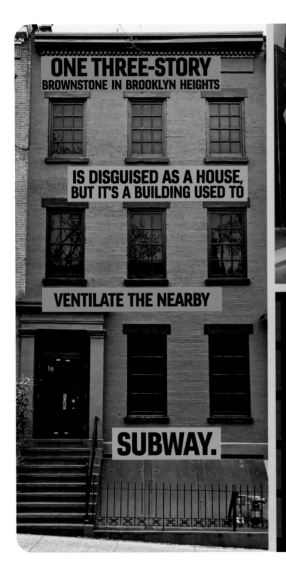

ONE THREE-STORY BROWNSTONE IN BROOKLYN HEIGHTS

IS DISGUISED AS A HOUSE, BUT IT'S A BUILDING USED TO

VENTILATE THE NEARBY

SUBWAY.

EVERY YEAR PEOPLE RUN A RACE UP THE 1,576 STAIRS OF THE EMPIRE STATE BUILDING TO REACH THE 86TH FLOOR.

If you walk **20 BLOCKS** (north-south) in New York City, you've walked **ONE MILE** (1.6 km).

Manhattan's **One World Trade Center,** the tallest building in the United States, **has 71 elevators.**

34

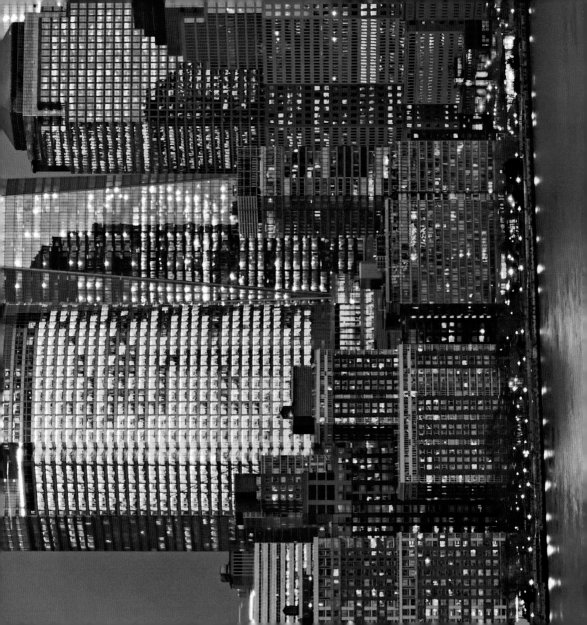

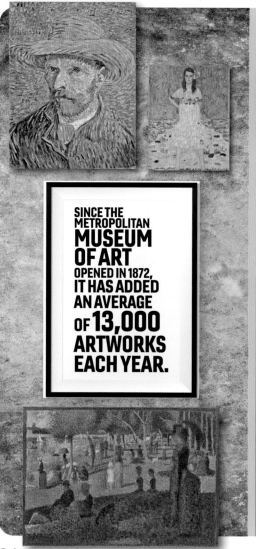

SINCE THE METROPOLITAN MUSEUM OF ART OPENED IN 1872, IT HAS ADDED AN AVERAGE OF 13,000 ARTWORKS EACH YEAR.

THE AVERAGE NEW YORK CITY TAXI TRAVELS 70,000 MILES (113,000 KM) PER YEAR.

More than **65 million people** visit New York City in a year.

A secret staircase inside the Washington Square Arch leads to the rooftop.

THE ROCKETTE DANCERS DO MORE THAN **160 HIGH KICKS** PER SHOW.

THERE ARE *TINY MICROPHONES* IN THE HEELS OF THEIR SHOES.

SNOOPY HAS APPEARED IN THE MACY'S THANKSGIVING DAY PARADE MORE THAN ANY OTHER CHARACTER.

THE MAGICIAN HARRY HOUDINI IS BURIED IN MACHPELAH CEMETERY IN QUEENS, AND A "BROKEN WAND" CEREMONY TAKES PLACE THERE EVERY YEAR TO HONOR HIM.

There are more than **119,000 hotel rooms** in the city.

The City Hall subway stop in New York City was built with skylights and chandeliers.

The first paved road in the United States built specially for cars—the Long Island Motor Parkway—opened in Queens in 1908.

New York's mass transit system includes **6,418** subway cars.

41

Thomas Edison invented super-durable cement that was used to build the original **Yankee Stadium,** which was torn down in 2009.

The borough of **Queens** is named after an actual queen—Catherine of Braganza, who married King Charles II of England.

TWO DAYS A YEAR, ON WHAT IS CALLED MANHATTANHENGE, **THE SUN SETS** EXACTLY ALIGNED WITH MANHATTAN'S STREET GRID.

A 2018 SURVEY COUNTED 2,373 EASTERN GRAY SQUIRRELS IN CENTRAL PARK.

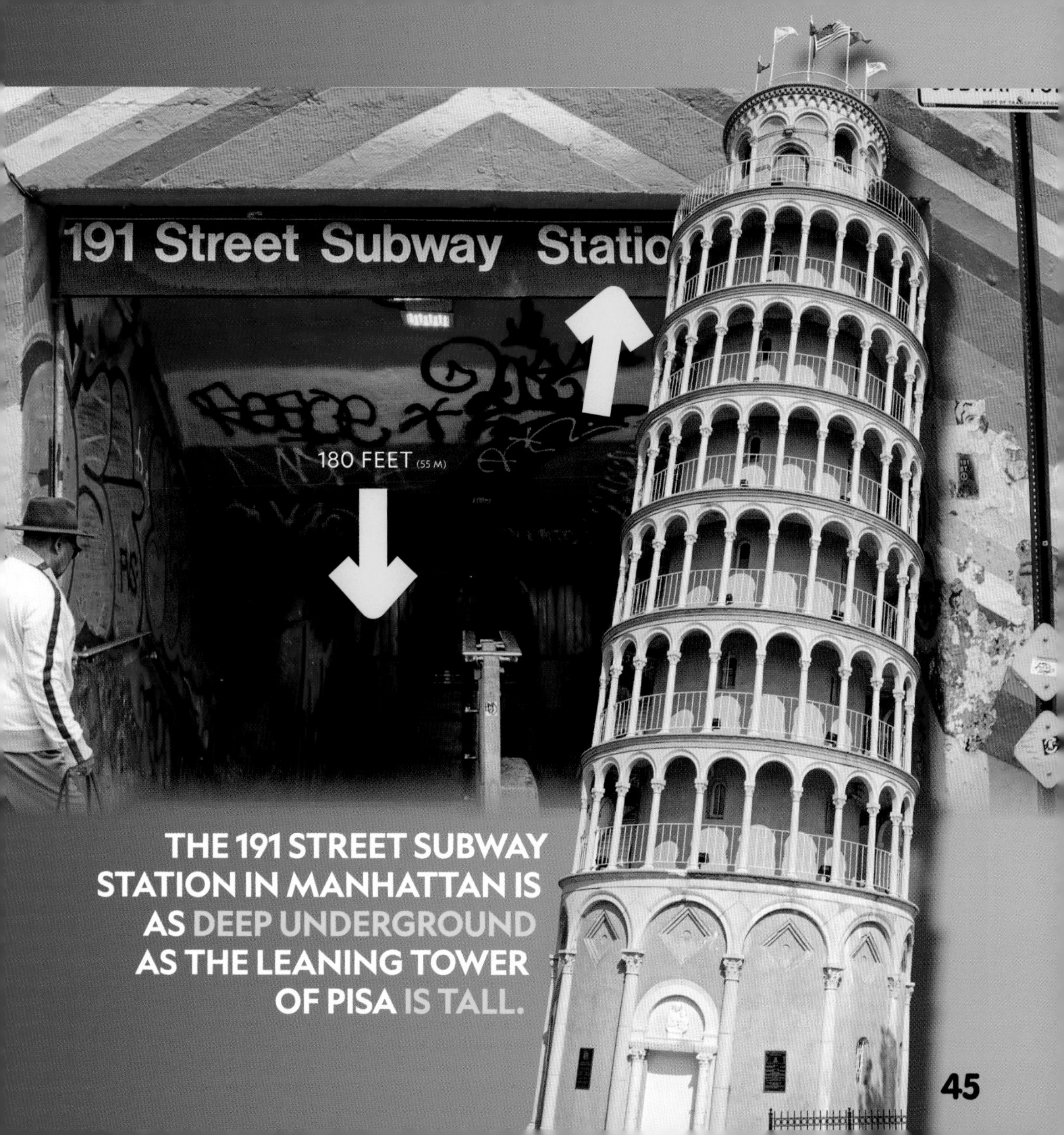

191 Street Subway Station

180 FEET (55 M)

THE 191 STREET SUBWAY STATION IN MANHATTAN IS AS DEEP UNDERGROUND AS THE LEANING TOWER OF PISA IS TALL.

Hundreds of humpback whales swim through New York Harbor every year.

If you took all the subway tracks and laid them out in a line, they

would stretch from New York City to Chicago, Illinois, U.S.A.

FLOWER ARRANGEMENTS FOR SPECIAL EVENTS AT THE METROPOLITAN MUSEUM OF ART CAN BE AS TALL AS A TWO-STORY BUILDING.

New York residents throw out about six billion pounds (2.7 billion kg) of trash a year.

Backyard chickens are **LEGAL IN THE CITY**, but **ROOSTERS ARE NOT ALLOWED.**

THE FIRST AERIAL **COMMUTER CABLE CAR** IN NORTH AMERICA CONNECTS MANHATTAN'S EAST SIDE TO **ROOSEVELT ISLAND** IN THE EAST RIVER.

THE MARBLE LIONS IN FRONT OF THE NEW YORK PUBLIC LIBRARY ARE NICKNAMED PATIENCE & FORTITUDE.

Emily Warren Roebling oversaw construction of the **Brooklyn Bridge** and was the first person to ride across it, carrying a **rooster in her lap** for good luck.

That's weird!

50

To show that the bridge was **safe,** showman P. T. Barnum paraded **21 elephants and 17 camels** across it on May 17, 1884, a week before it opened.

Some New Yorkers call the red meat sauce that you put on pasta "gravy."

IN THE 1990S, THE BOROUGH OF STATEN ISLAND VOTED **TO LEAVE THE CITY.** (BUT IT NEVER HAPPENED.)

Instead of **giant balloons,** the first Macy's Thanksgiving Day Parade in 1924 had **elephants and tigers** from the Central Park Zoo.

It takes **90 people** to control the largest balloons in the Macy's **Thanksgiving Day Parade.**

The *Apatosaurus* balloon in the parade is **life-size.**

That's weird!

The ball that drops in Times Square to ring in the new year weighs as much as **15 large grizzly bears.**

The ball's **32,256 LED lights** can create billions of colorful patterns.

NOT TO SCALE

AN ICE-CREAM SHOP IN BROOKLYN

SOMETIMES SERVES OLIVE OIL ICE CREAM.

The nickname **Big Apple** took off when a reporter used the term, which means "the best of its kind," to describe the city's horse-racing circuit.

The **KNICKS** NBA team got its name from the **KNICKER-BOCKER** style of pants worn by early **Dutch settlers.**

ABOUT **HALF THE HORSES** THAT NEW YORK'S POLICE OFFICERS RIDE **LIVE IN A STABLE** ON THE GROUND FLOOR OF A **LUXURY APARTMENT BUILDING** IN MANHATTAN.

NEW YORK POLICE HAVE TWO MOBILE BLACKSMITH VANS TO REPLACE HORSESHOES RIGHT **ON CITY STREETS,** EVEN IN TIMES SQUARE.

At least 42 different species of ants live in New York City.

NEW YORK CITY HAS NEARLY **20 "SUPERTALL" SKYSCRAPERS**

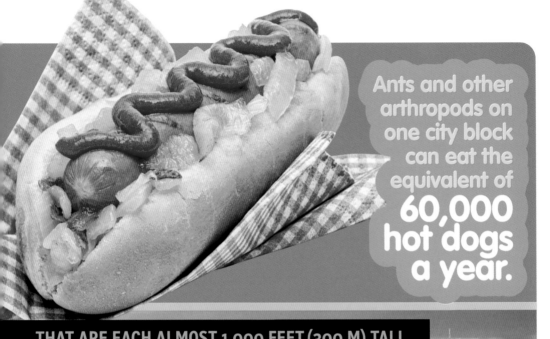

Ants and other arthropods on one city block can eat the equivalent of **60,000 hot dogs a year.**

THAT ARE EACH ALMOST 1,000 FEET (300 M) TALL.

The biodegradable **confetti** that falls during the Times Square New Year's celebration weighs **3,000 pounds** (1,360 kg).

It takes **100 people** to throw it over the crowd.

At the "**WISHING WALL**," you can write wishes on the pieces of confetti that will be thrown.

It's illegal for kangaroos, hippos, and rhinos to perform tricks in the city.

New York City
used to be called
New Amsterdam.

THE QUEENS MUSEUM INCLUDES A 9,335-SQUARE-FOOT (867-SQ-M) MODEL OF THE CITY'S FIVE BOROUGHS.

SOME PEOPLE HEAR THE **FIRST THREE NOTES OF "SOMEWHERE,"** A SONG FROM THE MUSICAL *WEST SIDE STORY,* WHEN CERTAIN SUBWAY TRAINS LEAVE THE STATION.

A bird rehab center in Manhattan teaches New Yorkers how to foster an injured pigeon—including offering a **"buddy bird"** for it to bond with.

The city is home to the largest urban zoo in the United States—the **BRONX ZOO.**

More than **70 SNOW LEOPARD CUBS** have been born at the Bronx Zoo.

The zoo houses some **50,000 HISSING COCKROACHES,** which can grow to be more than three inches (8 cm) long.

You can name a hissing cockroach for a **LOVED ONE FOR VALENTINE'S DAY.**

You can buy a **rainbow-colored bagel** at a Brooklyn bakery and add a **cotton candy spread.**

Rats in the subway system have been seen carrying pizza slices and coffee cups.

VISUAL-RECOGNITION SOFTWARE AT THE **AMERICAN KENNEL CLUB MUSEUM OF THE DOG** MATCHES YOU WITH THE DOG BREED THAT LOOKS MOST LIKE YOU.

A public bathroom in a curbside kiosk in central Manhattan is decorated with **SEASONAL PLANTS** and plays **classical music.**

At the Play Fair Convention and Expo in Manhattan, a 12-year-old girl set a record by making the **WORLD'S LARGEST BATCH OF PURPLE SLIME,** which weighed 13,820 pounds (6,269 kg).

In 2019, a New York City jewelry company made a **diamond-tipped gold dreidel** valued at **$70,000.**

MMUSEUMM IS A TINY MUSEUM HOUSED IN A FREIGHT ELEVATOR THAT OPENS ONTO A MANHATTAN STREET.

THE WORLD'S **FIRST ESCALATOR** WAS CREATED AS AN AMUSEMENT PARK RIDE AT **CONEY ISLAND** IN 1895.

The **Harlem Globetrotters** got their start in Chicago, Illinois, U.S.A., in 1927.

They didn't play a game in Harlem until more than **40 years later.**

Exterior movie scenes of the *Ghostbusters* headquarters were filmed at a working firehouse in Manhattan.

·8·HOOK & LADDER·8·

F.D. N.Y.

8

A NEW YORK CITY RESTAURANT SOLD A CHEESECAKE FOR

$5,000.

IT CONTAINED CHEESE MADE FROM **WATER BUFFALO MILK** AND **WHITE TRUFFLES** FROM ITALY.

73

On the **SeaGlass Carousel** in Battery Park, riders take a spin on color-changing fiberglass fish.

The carousel's exterior is modeled after a **nautilus shell.**

Mosaics of dressed-up Weimaraner dogs were on display at a Manhattan subway station.

A MAN SET A RECORD BY EATING ALL THE CHOCOLATES FROM AN ADVENT CALENDAR IN 1 MINUTE 28 SECONDS IN NEW YORK CITY.

OFFICES INSIDE A 12-STORY MANHATTAN BUILDING OVERLOOK A **SUBTROPICAL FOREST** THAT GROWS IN THE LOBBY.

In 2018, two goats wandered onto train tracks in Brooklyn, holding up commuter traffic.

That's weird!

The giant boulders in **Central Park** were once embedded in glaciers that melted in New York **18,000 years ago.**

A New York City floral designer uses city garbage cans as giant vases for public flower displays.

AN ART GALLERY IN MANHATTAN SPECIALIZES IN 19TH-CENTURY DOG PAINTINGS AND WELCOMES PETS ON LEASHES.

The corner of West 63rd Street and Broadway was renamed **Sesame Street** in honor of the TV show.

A 10-story light display transformed the outside of a Manhattan department store to look like the castle from *Frozen.*

Architect Frank Lloyd Wright wanted the walls of his Solomon R. **Guggenheim Museum** to mimic the **tilt of an easel** in order to best display artworks.

Museum staff paint over scuffs on the interior walls nearly every day.

The famous spiral ramp of the museum is more than a quarter mile (0.4 km) long.

ALBERTO BURRI

THE WINNING PUP AT THE WESTMINSTER DOG SHOW DOESN'T WIN ANY PRIZE MONEY, BUT IT DOES GET TO **EAT A MEAL AT A FANCY NEW YORK CITY RESTAURANT.**

A dozen giant illuminated seesaws were placed in the middle of a street in Manhattan's Garment District as part of an interactive art exhibit.

AT THE BROOKLYN SUPERHERO SUPPLY STORE, YOU CAN BUY BOTTLES OF X-RAY VISION AND TRUTH SERUM.

The **chefs** at a restaurant on Staten Island are all **grandmas** who cook food **honoring their cultures.**

The site of one Staten Island park used to be home to the **world's largest garbage dump.**

A four-story statue of a Dalmatian **balancing a taxi on its nose** sits outside a children's hospital in Manhattan.

THE EXTERIOR OF A LOCKSMITH BUSINESS IN GREENWICH VILLAGE IS COVERED IN **10,000** KEYS.

EVERY **FOURTH OF JULY,** CONTESTANTS RACE TO **EAT** AS **MANY HOT DOGS AS THEY CAN IN 10 MINUTES** AT NATHAN'S FAMOUS HOT DOG STAND IN CONEY ISLAND; THE RECORD IS 75.

NATHAN'S OFFERS CONTESTANTS **WATER TO DRINK,** BUT THEY CAN ALSO BRING ANY BEVERAGE OF THEIR CHOICE.

At an exhibit in Spyscape, a museum about spies, visitors try to get through a tunnel while avoiding a spiderweb of laser beams.

The Brooklyn Art Library has a collection of **41,000 sketchbooks** from artists **around the world.**

YOU CAN BUY A DIAMOND ENGAGEMENT RING FROM A VENDING MACHINE IN ROCKEFELLER CENTER.

Despite its name, Rat Island, a 2.5-acre (1-ha) private island in the Bronx, DOES NOT have any rats living on it.

Aw, rats!

Every year millions of **green bananas** are sent to a facility in the **Bronx** to ripen.

Pressurized rooms TRICK THE BANANAS into "thinking" they are back in their TROPICAL climate, turning them YELLOW.

When the "Mona Lisa" was displayed at the Metropolitan Museum of Art in 1963, it was only the second time it had left France. (The first was when it was stolen and taken to Italy.)

The American Museum of Natural History decorated a holiday tree with more than **800 folded-paper dinosaur models.**

In a two-week period in 1961, one New York Rangers hockey player **lost seven teeth on the ice.**

PHOTO COMPOSITE

96

Teenagers found an eight-foot (2.4-m)-long alligator in a Manhattan storm drain on February 9, 1935.

Some New Yorkers still celebrate February 9 as Alligators in the Sewers Day.

Where's my party hat?

From 2010 to 2019, 130,000 rat sightings were called in to New York City's help line.

Riders on board the Bug Carousel at the Bronx Zoo sit on one of 64 different types of insects.

IN WINTERTIME AT THE NEW YORK BOTANICAL GARDEN IN THE BRONX, A MODEL TRAIN PASSES THROUGH A DISPLAY OF 175 NEW YORK LANDMARKS.

DIRT FROM NEW JERSEY had to be brought in to **PLANT TREES** in Central Park when it was constructed in the **mid-1800s.**

The stuffed animals that belonged to author **A. A. Milne's son, Christopher Robin,** which inspired the ***Winnie-the-Pooh*** characters, are on display at the New York Public Library.

You can take a speedboat ride
to the Statue of Liberty.

A replica of a British World War I **fighter plane** sits on the roof of a Manhattan office building.

ONE HUNDRED YEARS AGO, WHAT IS TODAY LAGUARDIA AIRPORT WAS THE SITE OF AN AMUSEMENT PARK.

LaGuardia Airport

A SECTION OF THE

BERLIN WALL

STANDS IN

BATTERY PARK CITY.

Central Park's "Alice in Wonderland" was designed for children to climb on—the mushrooms serve as steps.

The winter of 1780 was **SO COLD** that NEW YORK HARBOR FROZE—

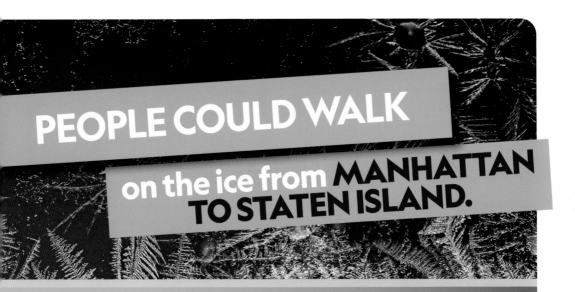

PEOPLE COULD WALK

on the ice from MANHATTAN TO STATEN ISLAND.

THE NEIGHBORHOOD OF
JAMAICA,
IN QUEENS, ISN'T NAMED
AFTER THE CARIBBEAN
COUNTRY—IT COMES FROM
THE ALGONQUIN INDIAN WORD FOR
BEAVER, *JAMECO*.

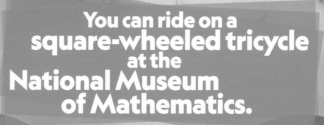

You can ride on a
square-wheeled tricycle
at the
**National Museum
of Mathematics.**

In 1973, the bronze "ugly duckling" accompanying the Hans Christian Andersen statue in Central Park was stolen, but it was later found in a scrapyard and reinstalled.

Puffed-rice cereal was invented at the New York Botanical Garden in 1901.

Wall Street, the center of Manhattan's Financial District, was named after an actual nine-foot (2.7-m)-tall wall that Dutch settlers built at the site.

EGG CREAMS, a New York City invention, include **neither eggs nor cream.**

GUESTS CAN SPEND THE NIGHT AT AN **ISOLATED**— AND RUMORED TO BE **HAUNTED**— **LIGHTHOUSE** IN LONG ISLAND SOUND.

PEOPLE CAN WALK AROUND A **MODEL** OF THE STATUE OF LIBERTY IN **PARIS, FRANCE,** THAT'S ONE-FOURTH THE SIZE OF **THE ORIGINAL.**

The first **public golf course** in the United States, Van Cortlandt Golf Course, opened in the Bronx on July 6, 1895.

AN ART MUSEUM IN MANHATTAN FEATURES A ROOM FILLED WITH DIRT.

That's my kind of art!

SCRABBLE WAS INVENTED IN QUEENS

FOSSILS ARE **EMBEDDED IN THE LIMESTONE FLOOR** OF GRAND CENTRAL STATION.

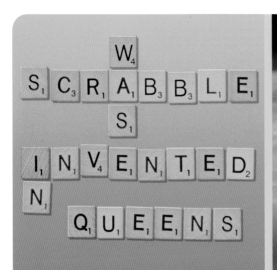

The American Museum of Natural History has the LARGEST METEORITE on display in the world.

IT TAKES **25 GALLONS (95 L) OF PAINT** TO COVER THE 94-FOOT (29-M)-LONG BLUE WHALE MODEL AT THE AMERICAN MUSEUM OF NATURAL HISTORY.

IN 2001, ARTISTS ADDED A
BELLY BUTTON
TO THE BLUE WHALE,
40 YEARS AFTER THE
MODEL WAS MADE.

Central Park's designers included only one **intentionally** **straight path** in the entire park.

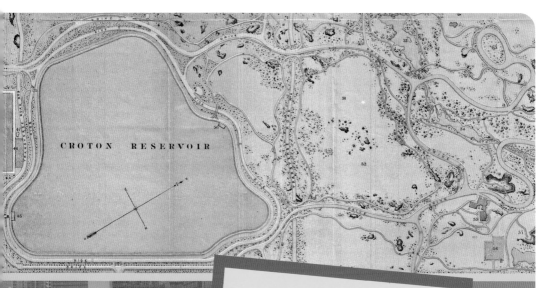

You can **always** catch the Staten Island Ferry—it **never** stops running.

The holiday tree at **Rockefeller Center** is traditionally a **Norway spruce.**

The tree is **strung with 50,000 multicolored LED** lights.

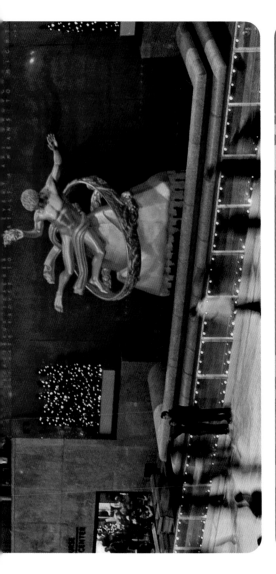

The wires for the lights would stretch five miles (8 km).

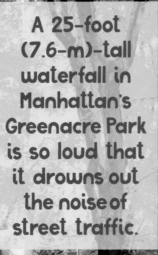

A 25-foot (7.6-m)-tall waterfall in Manhattan's Greenacre Park is so loud that it drowns out the noise of street traffic.

SIDEWALKS IN NEW YORK CITY ARE PAINTED THE COLOR "BATTLESHIP GRAY."

In the 1920s, tides washed away a sunbathing hot spot known as Hog Island off the coast of Far Rockaway, in Queens.

Some 25 species of sharks, including **great whites,** swim off New York City's coastline.

New York City's fire department helped make **Dalmatians** **famous** as firehouse dogs when they **started using** **them** in the 1870s.

People have accidentally left a wedding veil, $20,000 worth of gold bars, a classical violin worth $4 million, and a robot in the back seats of city taxis.

A pneumatic tube system once connected 23 city post offices, sending letters back and forth at 30 miles an hour (48 km/h).

The Edge at Hudson Yards, a 1,131-foot (345-m)-high observation deck, has glass floors and an outdoor staircase connecting the 100th and 101st floors.

You can lean on one of the 79 nine-foot (2.7-m)-tall glass panels that angle outward for a sky-high view.

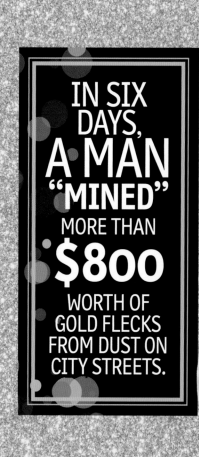

IN SIX DAYS, A MAN "MINED" MORE THAN $800 WORTH OF GOLD FLECKS FROM DUST ON CITY STREETS.

Pedestrians had to pay to cross the city's first bridge, built in 1693, but British soldiers could cross it for free.

Ray's Pizza, Original Ray's Pizza, Real Ray's, and Original Famous Ray's Pizza have all been different pizza restaurants.

At the **FAO Schwarz toy store,** you can build your own remote-control car with the help of a "mechanic."

The French bulldog is the city's most popular dog breed.

HOUSES ON A BLOCK IN BROOKLYN HAVE FOUR-FOOT (1.2-M)-TALL "HOBBIT-SIZE" ENTRANCE DOORS.

A three-story-tall sewing needle "threads" a 14-foot (4.3-m)-long button in Manhattan's Garment District.

Nineteen official signs misspell the name of the **Verrazzano-Narrows Bridge** (the second z is missing) and are slowly being replaced.

A MOTOROLA ENGINEER WALKING ON SIXTH AVENUE MADE THE *FIRST EVER CELL PHONE CALL* ON APRIL 3, 1973.

ADULTS AREN'T ALLOWED at one comic book store in Brooklyn unless they come in **WITH A KID.**

That's weird!

In 2019, one of the trendiest dog names in New York City was "Chicken."

IF YOU UNWOUND THE STEEL STRANDS THAT SUPPORT THE GEORGE WASHINGTON BRIDGE, THEY WOULD STRETCH AROUND THE WORLD FOUR TIMES.

TICK TOCK TICK TOCK TOCK CK TIC DO TIC TOC TICK TOCK TICK

A six-foot (2-m)-tall cuckoo clock at the FAO Schwarz toy store was silenced after a neighboring store complained about the noise.

THE 36 CREATURES AT THE **TOTALLY KID CAROUSEL** IN HARLEM COME FROM KIDS' IMAGINATIONS—THEIR ORIGINAL SKETCHES HANG ABOVE EACH ANIMAL.

Ellis Island's hospital had curved, Y-shaped corridors— contagious patients were sent to the right and noncontagious patients to the left.

If you walked every trail in Central Park, you'd walk 58 miles (93 km).

CENTRAL PARK IS AS BIG AS

614

AMERICAN FOOTBALL FIELDS.

TWO **WINGED HELMETS** HANG FROM THE CORNERS OF THE **CHRYSLER BUILDING'S** 31ST FLOOR, REPLICAS OF LATE 1920S CHRYSLER CAR HOOD ORNAMENTS.

In 1974, a man walked on a tightrope stretched between the two towers of the World Trade Center.

New York City inventor **Thomas Adams** was the **first person** to manufacture chewing gum, selling it in vending machines at subway stations in 1888.

The spire of the New York Life Building is covered in

25,000 gold-leaf tiles.

BROADWAY IS THE **LONGEST STREET** IN MANHATTAN, STRETCHING **13 MILES** (21 KM).

Old iron manhole covers in New York City have **raised patterns** on them that once kept horses and carriages from slipping.

The 120-foot (37-m) stainless-steel Unisphere, located in a Queens park, is the largest model of the world.

Lin-Manuel Miranda wrote two songs for his musical *Hamilton* from Aaron Burr's bedroom in the oldest house in Manhattan, the **Morris-Jumel Mansion.**

Some say that the ghost of Aaron Burr's wife, **Eliza Jumel,** haunts the house.

Almost all Broadway theaters lack a row I.

Row I is skipped so that people don't mistakenly think that they are in row 1 (one).

That's weird!

Astronauts can see the lights of Times Square from the International Space Station.

"MIDNIGHT MOMENT" IS A DIGITAL ART EXHIBITION THAT APPEARS ON ELECTRIC BILLBOARDS IN TIMES SQUARE EVERY NIGHT FROM 11:57 P.M. TO MIDNIGHT.

The Little Red Lighthouse, Manhattan Island's only remaining lighthouse, is located under the George Washington Bridge.

THE THEATER SECTION OF BROADWAY WAS ONCE CALLED THE GREAT WHITE WAY because it was one of the first streets in the United States to be lit up with white electric lights.

An 18-foot (5.5-m)-tall **peacock** made of **blue flowers** and shrubs and covered in **11,000** blue lights was on display at Rockefeller Center in 2020.

AS MANY AS **10,000** **PEOPLE AN HOUR** VIEW MACY'S HOLIDAY WINDOW DISPLAYS IN PEAK SEASON.

IT TAKES 21 DAYS TO INSTALL THEM.

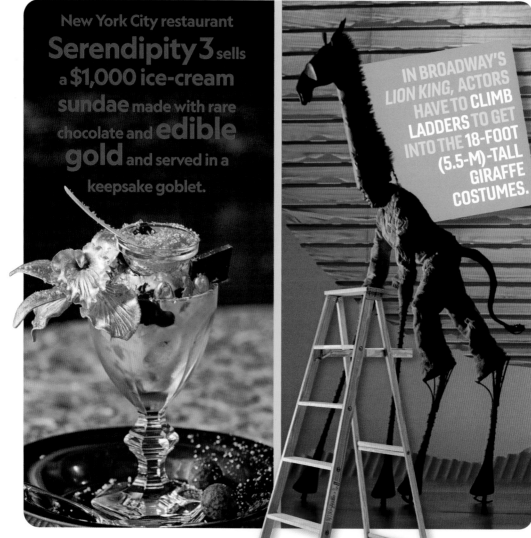

New York City restaurant **Serendipity 3** sells a **$1,000 ice-cream sundae** made with rare chocolate and **edible gold** and served in a keepsake goblet.

IN BROADWAY'S LION KING, ACTORS HAVE TO CLIMB LADDERS TO GET INTO THE 18-FOOT (5.5-M)-TALL GIRAFFE COSTUMES.

A musician created a **sound sculpture** in Times Square—the sound of **low-pitched church bells** echoes through a street grate 24 hours a day.

TIMES SQUARE IS NOT A SQUARE—IT'S SHAPED LIKE A BOW TIE.

For the 50th anniversary of the 1933 movie **King Kong,** an 84-foot (26-m)-tall inflatable gorilla was attached to the side of the Empire State Building.

It took handlers **10 days** to get the **3,000-pound** (1,360-kg) gorilla settled on his perch.

For more than 25 years, **artist Hani Shihada** has used New York City **sidewalks as canvases** to make drawings with **chalk and pastels.**

THE *NEW YORK POST* WAS FOUNDED IN 1801 BY **ALEXANDER HAMILTON.**

Before a wintertime flight, you can ice-skate at Runway Rink, located on the tarmac at John F. Kennedy International Airport.

The children's book *The Snowy Day* has been checked out of the New York Public Library system more than any other book.

The **Coney Island Polar Bear Club** hosts the annual New Year's Day Plunge, when swimmers jump into the frigid Atlantic Ocean.

The Metropolitan Transportation Authority will email you a "late letter" if your train delay makes you late for work or school.

Some New Yorkers **PAY DOG WALKERS** to take their pups to the **countryside so they can run off-leash.**

In 2017, a bronze statue known as the "Fearless Girl" was unveiled to STARE DOWN Wall Street's "Charging Bull" statue.

The **artist** who created the famous **7,000-pound (3,175-kg) bronze bull** first placed it in front of the New York Stock Exchange **illegally.**

Frozen custard was invented at Coney Island in 1919, when two brothers added eggs to their ice-cream recipe, causing the mixture to thicken and melt slower.

They sold more than 18,000 cones the first weekend.

DURING THE U.S. CIVIL WAR, JEWELRY STORE TIFFANY & CO. MADE SWORDS FOR THE UNION ARMY.

NO PARKING
Anytime

NEW YORK DRIVERS SPEND AN AVERAGE OF 107 HOURS A YEAR LOOKING FOR A PARKING SPOT.

When it first opened in 1927, the Coney Island Cyclone roller coaster cost 25 cents to ride.

(Today it costs $10.)

In 1977, a man set a world record by riding the Cyclone continuously for 104 hours.

159

The famous Central Park restaurant Tavern on the Green was originally designed to house 700 sheep.

The locker rooms at Madison Square Garden are round so that players can see each other during team meetings.

FOR MORE THAN 20 YEARS, **AN ARTIST FROM BROOKLYN** HAS DRESSED IN **BRIGHT GREEN EVERY DAY**—AND EVEN DYES HER HAIR TO MATCH.

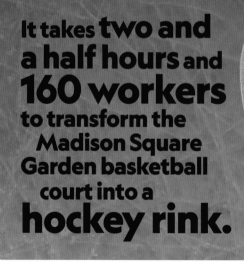

It takes **two and a half hours** and **160 workers** to transform the Madison Square Garden basketball court into a **hockey rink.**

Seven concrete domes at a park in Queens are arranged to represent phases of the **moon.**

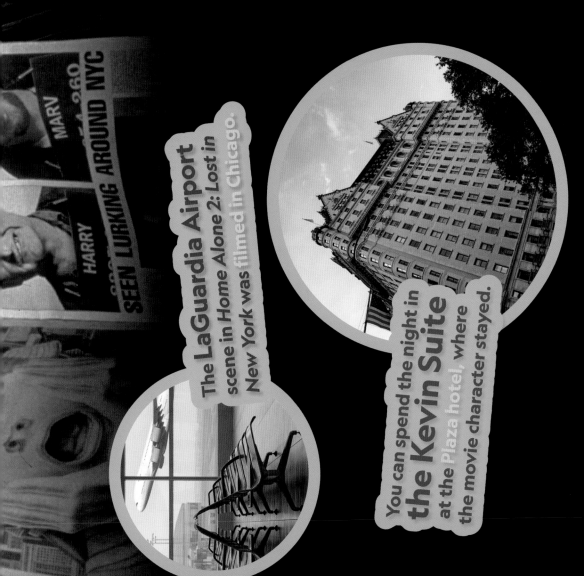

MARV   HARRY

SEEN LURKING AROUND NYC

The LaGuardia Airport scene in *Home Alone 2: Lost in New York* was filmed in Chicago.

You can spend the night in **the Kevin Suite** at the Plaza hotel, where the movie character stayed.

Diners at the famous **Katz's Delicatessen** get a ticket with their order number—and are **charged $50** if they **lose it.**

SINGER **KATY PERRY** ONCE ATTENDED NEW YORK'S MET **GALA** DRESSED AS A **CHANDELIER.**

IT TAKES NEW YORK CITY BAKER DOMINIQUE ANSEL THREE DAYS TO MAKE HIS SIGNATURE **CRONUT,** WHICH IS A CROSS BETWEEN A **CROISSANT** AND A **DOUGHNUT.**

167

The Rose Main Reading Room at the New York Public Library is as long as two city blocks.

DATE DUE

OVERDUE

PUBLIC LIBRARY

A book that President George Washington checked out from a New York City library was returned 221 years late.

A **VENOMOUS EGYPTIAN COBRA** WENT MISSING FROM ITS BRONX ZOO ENCLOSURE IN 2011—AND WASN'T FOUND UNTIL **SEVEN DAYS LATER.**

Garbage

of New York City™

100% authentic
HAND-PICKED from the fertile streets of NY, NY
www.nycgarbage.com
© 2009 New York City Garbage

Garb

of New York Ci

100% authentic
HAND-PICKED from the fe
www.nycgarbage.com
© 2009 New York City Garbage

More than 1,300 cubes have been

Garbage
of New York City™

100% authentic
HAND-PICKED from the fertile streets of NY, NY
www.nycgarbage.com

© 2009 New York City Garbage

ge

treets of NY, NY

A MANHATTAN ARTIST MAKES PAINTINGS INSPIRED BY NEW YORK CITY'S MANHOLE COVERS.

In 2012

Chilly and Baby Hope

tied the knot in a $270,000 doggie wedding to raise money for the Humane Society of New York.

The number of visitors to the
**American Museum of
Natural History** increased
by 20 percent within 10 days of the
Night at the Museum movie release.

That's weird!

Parts of **FIVE MEDIEVAL ABBEYS** were dismantled in Europe and reassembled in northern Manhattan to become part of the **MET CLOISTERS** museum.

At Ellen's Stardust Diner, waitstaff sing and dance while delivering food to customers.

KIDS FROM MORE THAN 60 COUNTRIES DONATED MEDALS AND COINS TO CREATE THE PEACE BELL AT THE UNITED NATIONS HEADQUARTERS, WHICH IS USUALLY RUNG ONLY TWICE A YEAR.

PART OF MANHATTAN'S NINTH AVENUE IS NAMED **OREO WAY** IN HONOR OF THE COOKIE, WHICH WAS INVENTED AT A **NABISCO FACTORY** ON THE STREET IN 1912.

For professional **bull riders** to compete in Madison Square Garden, some 750 tons (680 t) of dirt is added to the arena floor.

AT THE MURRAY HILL STREET FESTIVAL, YOU CAN SNAP A PHOTO WITH PEOPLE DRESSED AS HISTORICAL LOCAL FIGURES SUCH AS ARTIST ANDY WARHOL AND ABRAHAM LINCOLN'S GRANDDAUGHTER.

From the 1960s through the '80s, **"swimmobiles"**— pools attached to trucks— traveled through the city to offer kids a dip on hot summer days.

A Mexican restaurant in Manhattan creates a cheesy 16-layer taco tower with 20 tortillas.

Two bronze owls perched on a monument in Herald Square have blinking eyes that glow an eerie green at night.

A restaurant in Manhattan offers **chicken wings dusted in 24-karat gold flakes.**

At 2,765 acres (1,119 ha), **Pelham Bay Park** in the Bronx is more than **three times larger** than Central Park.

Hot weather causes the steel cables on the Verrazzano-Narrows Bridge to expand, making the double-decker bridge 12 feet (3.7 m) lower in the summer than in the winter.

SIXTEEN PUGS—
EACH WITH A HEART-SHAPED BALLOON—HELPED A MAN PROPOSE IN CENTRAL PARK.

Slide Hill on Governors Island is home to a three-story slide — the tallest slide in New York City.

The hills on Governors Island were created with enough dirt and rock to fill 1,806 subway cars.

At the **Museum of the Moving Image** in Queens, you can visit **Jim Henson's** famous puppets, including Elmo, Kermit the Frog, Big Bird, and Miss Piggy.

The **Metropolitan Museum of Art** has collected as much as **$3,000 a year** in coins tossed into its fountains.

POWERED BY WATER PRESSURE, THE ORIGINAL ELEVATORS IN THE **FLATIRON BUILDING** WOULD REGULARLY **FLOOD.**

In 2019, a 16-year-old girl **swam 28.5 miles (45 km) around Manhattan Island in nine hours** to raise money for charity.

In 1965, teenagers stole a penguin from the New York Aquarium at Coney Island.

(It was returned safely.)

Spaghetti and meatballs was created in Little Italy.

FROM 1876 TO 1882, THE STATUE OF LIBERTY'S ARM AND TORCH WERE DISPLAYED IN MADISON SQUARE PARK TO RAISE MONEY FOR BUILDING THE STATUE'S PEDESTAL.

At the **FAO Schwarz toy store,** you can play music by jumping on **a giant floor keyboard.**

The New York Yankees have won the most World Series of any Major League Baseball team—

27.

No words are spoken in performances by **Blue Man Group**– they communicate only through gestures and sound.

They use **385 marshmallows,** **40 PIECES** of white chocolate, and **eight boxes of cereal** each week for their shows.

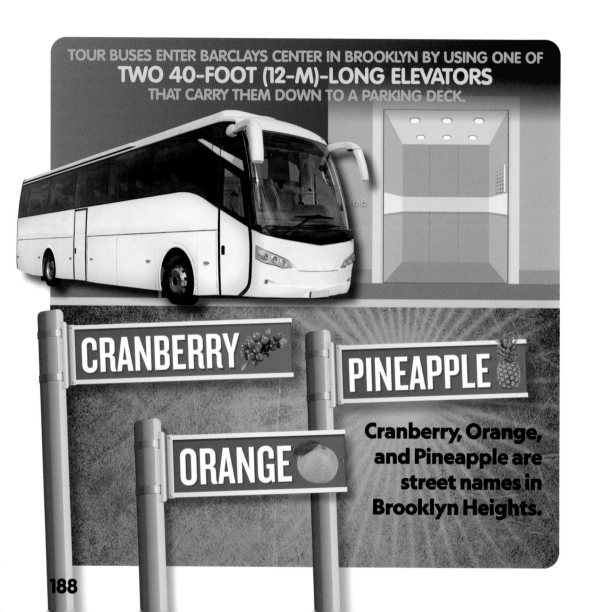

TOUR BUSES ENTER BARCLAYS CENTER IN BROOKLYN BY USING ONE OF
TWO 40-FOOT (12-M)-LONG ELEVATORS
THAT CARRY THEM DOWN TO A PARKING DECK.

CRANBERRY

PINEAPPLE

ORANGE

Cranberry, Orange, and Pineapple are street names in Brooklyn Heights.

Some **160 wild turkeys** caused so much mayhem in Staten Island—snatching hot dogs out of kids' hands and stopping traffic—that they were relocated upstate.

IN 2019, A **PEREGRINE FALCON PAIR** NICKNAMED **ADELE AND FRANK** RAISED THREE NESTLINGS ON A LEDGE ON THE 14TH FLOOR OF 55 WATER STREET IN MANHATTAN— ALL LIVESTREAMED.

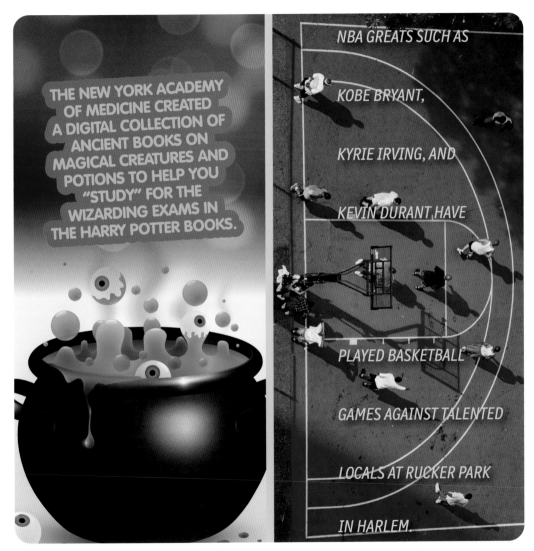

THE NEW YORK ACADEMY OF MEDICINE CREATED A DIGITAL COLLECTION OF ANCIENT BOOKS ON MAGICAL CREATURES AND POTIONS TO HELP YOU "STUDY" FOR THE WIZARDING EXAMS IN THE HARRY POTTER BOOKS.

NBA GREATS SUCH AS KOBE BRYANT, KYRIE IRVING, AND KEVIN DURANT HAVE PLAYED BASKETBALL GAMES AGAINST TALENTED LOCALS AT RUCKER PARK IN HARLEM.

191

Every year, the **CAT FILM FESTIVAL** showcases two hours of the best short films about kitties.

ONE DESIGN FOR THE HIGH LINE, AN ELEVATED FORMER TRAIN TRACK THAT'S NOW A CITY PARK IN MANHATTAN, INCLUDED A ONE-MILE (1.6-KM)-LONG SWIMMING POOL.

IN THE 1800s, MEN RODE HORSES IN FRONT OF FREIGHT TRAINS TRAVELING ON CITY STREETS TO WARN PEDESTRIANS OF ONCOMING TRAINS.

YOU CAN STILL SEE SAW MARKS ON THE FENCE POSTS IN NEW YORK CITY'S OLDEST PUBLIC PARK, BOWLING GREEN, FROM WHEN REVOLUTIONARIES CUT OFF THE ENGLISH CROWNS IN 1776.

In 1901, people paid five cents to sit in cushioned rocking chairs—instead of on hard park benches—in several city parks.

194

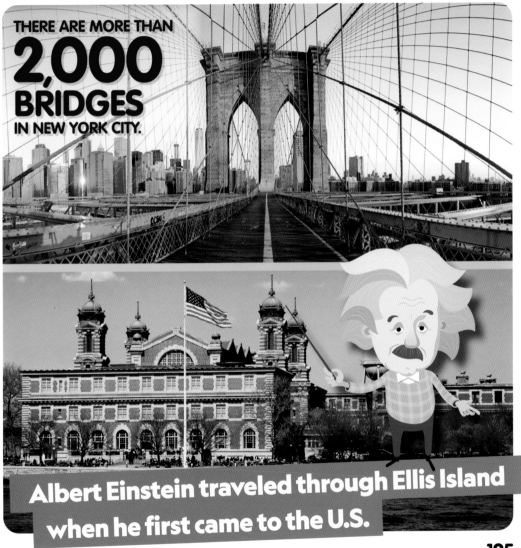

THERE ARE MORE THAN
2,000 BRIDGES IN NEW YORK CITY.

Albert Einstein traveled through Ellis Island when he first came to the U.S.

Many locals have strong feelings about bagels—for example, **NEVER toast** a fresh one.

And blueberry or rainbow bagels?

FUHGEDDABOUDIT!

THE **BAY RUNWAY** AT JOHN F. KENNEDY INTERNATIONAL AIRPORT WAS AN APPROVED LANDING SITE FOR **NASA'S SPACE SHUTTLE.**

Hundreds of people throw pillows at each other in Washington Square Park every April on **International Pillow Fight Day.**

Boldface indicates illustrations.

Copyright © 2021 National Geographic Partners, LLC

All rights reserved. Reproduction of the whole or any part of the contents without written permission from the publisher is prohibited.

NATIONAL GEOGRAPHIC and Yellow Border Design are trademarks of the National Geographic Society, used under license.

Since 1888, the National Geographic Society has funded more than 14,000 research, conservation, education, and storytelling projects around the world. National Geographic Partners distributes a portion of the funds it receives from your purchase to National Geographic Society to support programs including the conservation of animals and their habitats. To learn more, visit natgeo.com/info.

For more information, visit nationalgeographic .com, call 1-877-873-6846, or write to the following address:

National Geographic Partners, LLC
1145 17th Street N.W.
Washington, DC 20036-4688 U.S.A.

For librarians and teachers: nationalgeographic .com/books/librarians-and-educators

More for kids from National Geographic: natgeokids.com

National Geographic Kids magazine inspires children to explore their world with fun yet educational articles on animals, science, nature, and more. Using fresh storytelling and amazing photography, *Nat Geo Kids* shows kids ages 6 to 14 the fascinating truth about the world—and why they should care. **kids.nationalgeographic.com/subscribe**

For rights or permissions inquiries, please contact National Geographic Books Subsidiary Rights: bookrights@natgeo.com

Designed by Eva Abscher-Schantz

Trade paperback ISBN: 978-1-4263-7232-2
Reinforced library binding ISBN: 978-1-4263-7233-9

The publisher would like to thank Julie Beer, author and researcher; Michelle Harris, author and researcher; Robin Palmer, fact-checker; Grace Hill, project manager; Kathryn Williams, project editor; Hilary Andrews, photo editor; and Anne LeongSon and Gus Tello, design production assistants.

Printed in China
21/PPS/1

PHOTO CREDITS

AS: Adobe Stock; GI: Getty Images; SS: Shutterstock

Cover (CTR), Tracy Decourcy/Dreamstime; (UP RT), stock-enjoy/SS; (Statue of Liberty), Steve Collender/SS; (sunglasses), sumire8/SS; (mouth), Wayhome Studio/AS; (pizza), I_Larsen/SS; (LO RT), Thomas Pajot/AS; spine (UP), Tracy Decourcy/Dreamstime; (LO), Thomas Pajot/AS; back cover, Alexey Astakhov/AS; 1 (UP), Tracy Decourcy/Dreamstime; 1 (LO), Thomas Pajot/AS; 2 (RT), Gagliardi Photography/SS; 2 (LE), Sanjaykj/Dreamstime; 3 (UP), Tracy Decourcy/Dreamstime; 3 (LO), Thomas Pajot/AS; 4 (LE), Aygul Bulté/AS; 4 (RT), ad_hominem/AS; 6 (UP), Alexander Limbach/SS; 6 (LO CTR), Patcharanan/AS; 6 (LO), serazetdinov/SS; 7 (UP), Holly Kuchera/SS; 7 (LO), AP/SS; 8-9, ItzaVU/SS; 10, Vanessa Carvalho/SS; 11 (LE), Don Mammoser/SS; 11 (RT), Jorge Salcedo/SS; 12, alex5711/SS; 12-13, Antonio Salaverry/SS; 13, The Buttolph Collection of Menus, Rare Book Division, The New York Public Library; 14 (LE), Paul Maguire/SS; 14 (RT), freshidea/AS; 15 (UP), Alexander Lukatskiy/SS; 15 (LO), Joecho-16/GI; 16-17, tommk/AS; 17, Vaclav Volrab/SS; 18 (UP), Alexander Lukatskiy/SS; 18 (LO), Universal History Archive/SS; 19 (UP LE), Alexander Limbach/SS; 19 (UP RT), Turgay Malikli/SS; 19 (LO), clu/GI; 20, Willee Cole/AS; 20-21, Erika Cross/SS; 21, Javier Brosch/SS; 22 (UP), ggTravelDiary/SS; 22 (LO), rcfotostock/AS; 22 (INSET), Nathan Congleton/NBCU Photo Bank/NBCUniversal via GI; 23 (UP), elbud/SS; 23 (LO), Dzha/AS; 24, Craig Ruttle/AP Photo; 25 (UP LE), Craig Ruttle/AP Photo; 25 (UP CTR & LO LE), Felix Lipov/SS; 25 (RT), Craig Ruttle/AP Photo; 26 (UP LE), Roberto Borea/AP/SS; 26 (RT), Patti McConville/Alamy Stock Photo; 27 (UP), Thomas Hecker/AS; 27 (LO), Jack Vartoogian/GI; 28, Bokehboo Studios/SS; 29 (UP), Paolo Bona/SS; 29 (LO), a katz/SS; 30-31, Anthony Behar/Sipa via AP Images; 32 (UP), Henry S. Dziekan III/GI; 32 (LO), Gregory Pace/BEI/SS; 33 (LE), Fabrizio Ellis; 33 (RT), Adam Nadel/AP/SS; 34-35, haveseen/SS; 36 (LE), trigga/iStockphoto; 36 (UP LE), Bequest of Miss Adelaide Milton de Groot (1876-1967), 1967/Metropolitan Museum of Art; 36 (UP CTR), Gift of André and Clara Mertens, in memory of her mother, Jenny Pulitzer Steiner, 1964/Metropolitan Museum of Art; 36 (UP RT), Joe Ravi/SS; 36 (CTR LE), Kaikoro/AS; 36 (LO LE), Bequest of Sam A. Lewisohn, 1951/ Metropolitan Museum of Art; 37, jonbilous/AS; 38, Aaron Foster/GI; 38, Dave Allocca/Starpix/SS; 40 (UP), Carlo Allegri/Reuters/AS; 40 (LO LE), Everett Historical/SS; 40 (LO RT), S_E/SS; 41 (UP), Peter Praum/GI; 41 (LO LE), 3dsguru/iStockphoto; 41 (LO RT), Jan Krcmar/AS; 42 (UP), Popartic/SS; 42 (LO), Everett Historical/SS; 43, Joseph Sohm/SS; 44 (LE), Mihai_Andritoiu/SS; 44 (UP RT), Georgios Kollidas/AS; 44 (LO RT), Moose Henderson/Dreamstime; 45 (LE), William Volcov/SS; 45 (RT), rafalkrakow/GI; 46-47 (UP), wildestanimal/GI; 46-47 (LO), AndriyA/SS; 48 (LE), Dimitrios Kambouris/ MG18/GI for The Met Museum/Vogue; 48 (UP RT), kocetoiliev/SS; 48 (LO RT), Selenka/Dreamstime; 49 (UP), agsaz/SS; 49 (LO), Robert Sbarra/SS; 50 (CTR LE), Kamil Macniak/SS; 50 (CTR RT), Gift of Paul Roebling/Brooklyn Museum; 50 (LO LE), ananaline/AS; 50 (LO RT), Alexander Limbach/SS; 50–51, Songquan Deng/SS; 51 (UP LE), Martin Mecnarowski/SS; 51 (UP RT), Patryk Kosmider/AS; 52 (UP LE), Melica/SS; 52 (UP RT), grinchh/AS; 52 (LO LE), zlatovlaska2008/AS; 52 (LO RT), johavel/SS; 53 (background), Olga Rom/SS; 53 (UP), dpreezg/AS; 53 (LO LE), kinwun/AS; 53 (LO RT), Comaniciu Dan/SS; 54, NYC Russ/SS; 55, lev radin/SS; 56 (UP), Daria Rybakova/Dreamstime; 56 (LO), Nancy Ann Ellis/SS; 57 (UP LE), Lallapie/SS; 57 (UP RT), ChinHooi/SS; 57 (CTR RT), Issarawat Tattong/SS; 57 (LO LE), Designsstock/SS; 57 (LO RT), Archivist/AS; 58 (UP), Richard Drew/AP/SS; 58 (LO), Michael Nagle/The New York Times; 59 (UP), vovashevchuk/GI; 59 (LO), Richard Drew/AP/SS; 60, arlindo71/iStockphoto; 60-61, dibrova/SS; 61, Christopher Elwell/SS; 62, Simon Dux Media/SS; 63, Ben Archer/GI; 64 (UP LE), Eric Isselée/iStockphoto; 64 (CTR LE), Ondrej Prosicky/SS; 64 (LO LE), Isselee/Dreamstime; 64 (LO RT), Gustau Nacarino GN/Reuters/AS; 65 (UP LE), skochii/SS; 65 (UP CTR), 32 pixels/SS; 65 (UP RT), Moviestore/SS; 65 (LO), Perytskyy/AS; 66, belizar/SS; 66-67, littlenySTOCK/SS; 67, Chichinkin/SS; 68, Scot Rossillo/REX SS; 69 (LE), Antagain/GI; 69 (CTR), Bokehboo Studios/SS; 69 (CTR RT), olegganko/SS; 69 (RT), Gandee Vasan/GI; 69 (LO), Light House Media/SS; 70 (UP LE), Estate Diamond Jewelry; 70 (UP RT), Midorie/AS; 70 (LO RT), Robert K. Chin - Storefronts/Alamy Stock Photo; 71, FLHC 15/Alamy Stock Photo; 72, Ben Gabbe/GI; 73 (LE), Life In Pixels/SS; 73 (RT), Evgeny Karandaev/SS; 73 (UP RT), Nataliia Pyzhova/AS; 73 (CTR RT), Silvano Sarrocco/AS; 73 (LO RT), luca manieri/AS; 74, Timothy A. Clary/AFP via GI; 75, Brian Logan Photography/SS; 76 (LE), travelview/SS; 76 (UP RT), Eric Isselée/AS; 76 (LO CTR), Luseen/iStockphoto; 76 (LO RT), ESH/AS; 77 (UP), Linas T/SS; 77 (LO), Alexander Limbach/ SS; 78-79, tapanuth/AS; 80, Lewis Miller Design; 81 (UP LE), Javier Brosch/AS; 81 (CTR LE), Torsak Thammachote/SS; 81 (LO LE), GlobalP/GI; 81 (RT), Brett Carlsen/GI for Disney; 82 (LO), Torsak Thammachote/SS; 82, asiastock/SS; 83, Michele Falzone/GI; 84 (UP LE), 350jb/Dreamstime; 84 (UP RT), Seth Wenig/AP/SS; 84 (LO), Johannes Eisele/AFP via GI; 85, photoDISC; 86 (LE), Bigapplestock/ Dreamstime; 86 (UP RT), artbesouro/AS; 86 (LO RT), Ulrich Mueller/SS; 87, Paulette Sinclair/Alamy Stock Photo; 88-89, Hilary Andrews/NG Staff; 89, Digital Media Pro/SS; 90, Seth Wenig/AP/SS; 91 (LE), Belozorova Elena/AS; 91 (UP LE), Brand X; 91 (UP CTR), kentarcajuan/iStockphoto; 91 (UP RT), iarecottonstudio/SS; 91 (CTR RT), Alexander Limbach/SS; 91 (LO CTR), alexat25/SS; 91 (LO RT), Pakhnyushchyy/Dreamstime; 92, M Rutherford/SS; 93, ImLucky/AS; 94 (LE), susanne2688/AS; 94 (UP RT), Lornet/Dreamstime; 94 (RT), I. Pilon/SS; 95 (UP background), photoDISC; 95 (UP LE & CTR), Mandrixta/AS; 95 (UP RT), Raymond/AS; 95 (CTR LE), Cheattha/AS; 95 (CTR RT), DenisProduction/AS; 95 (LO), wowow/AS; 95 (LO background), francisblack/iStockphoto; 96, evenfh/SS; 96-97, terex/GI; 97 (LO LE), Alexander Limbach/SS; 97 (LO RT), dangdumrong/SS; 98, Antagain/GI; 99, Peter Bennett/ Danita Delimont/Alamy Stock Photo; 100 (UP LE), lev radin/SS; 100 (UP RT), Heather Shimmin/SS; 100 (LO), Fer Gregory/SS; 101, SS; 102 (LE), Merydolla/SS; 102 (UP RT), Alexander Limbach/SS; 102 (LO RT), Steve Collender/SS; 103, Lee Snider Photo Images/SS; 104 (LE), hugolacasse/SS; 104 (CTR), David Wall/Alamy Stock Photo; 104 (UP CTR), SimpLine/AS; 104 (UP RT), boscorelli/Shutterstock; 104 (LO RT), Evannovostro/SS; 105, Let Go Media/SS; 106, Frank Fichtmueller/SS; 106-107, Pasko Maksim/AS; 107, Richard Levine/Alamy Stock Photo; 108, Seth Wenig/AP/SS; 109 (LE), David L. Moore - US NE/Alamy Stock Photo; 109 (UP RT), pernsanitfoto/SS; 109 (CTR RT), mtphoto19/SS; 109 (LO RT), Bettmann/GI; 110 (LE), maxsol7/AS; 110 (RT), Roni/AS; 111, Franck Legros/AS; 112 (UP background), Erik1977/Dreamstime; 112 (UP RT), photoDISC; 112 (LO background), Madlen/SS; 112 (LO LE), Alexander Limbach/SS; 112 (LO RT), Dusty Cline/Dreamstime; 113 (UP LE), Chones/SS; 113 (LO LE), siimsepp/AS; 113 (RT), solarseven/SS; 114, J.J.Brown/AS; 114-115, Daniel Kreher/imageBROKER/SS; 115, J.J.Brown/AS; 116, Jennifer Griner/SS; 116-117 (UP), PicturePast/AS; 116-117 (LO), Christopher Penler/SS; 118, anfisa focusova/SS; 118-119, Andrew F. Kazmierski/SS; 119 (CTR), T.Sumaetho/SS; 119 (RT), Luseen/ iStockphoto; 120 (LE), Frances Roberts/Alamy Stock Photo; 120 (UP RT), pd studio/SS; 120 (LO RT), airmaria/AS; 121, wildestanimal/SS; 122 (LE), Christophe Testi/Dreamstime; 122 (RT), Susan Schmitz/ SS; 123 (UP LE), Thomas/AS; 123 (UP RT), CE Photography/SS; 123 (CTR LE), Ingram; 123 (CTR RT), julos/GI; 123 (LO), Simon Kadula/SS; 124-125, Gary Hershorn/GI; 126 (LE), surachet khamsuk/SS; 126 (CTR LE), T.Sumaetho/SS; 126 (UP RT), The Print Collector/Alamy Stock Photo; 126 (LO RT), Alexey Astakhov/AS; 127 (UP LE), gcafotografia/SS; 127 (UP RT), Jagodka/SS; 127 (LO LE), Randy Duchaine/ Alamy Stock Photo; 127 (LO RT), Eric Isselée/SS; 128 (LE), Joseph Perone/SS; 128 (LO LE), Warinthorn Krueangkham/Dreamstime; 128 (LO CTR), Andrea Danti/SS; 128 (LO RT), Timur Zima/SS; 129 (UP), eriksvoboda/AS; 129 (CTR LE), Alexander Limbach/SS; 129 (CTR RT), demphoto/AS; 129 (LO), Yummy Buum/AS; 130 (LE), stockphoto mania/SS; 130 (UP CTR), EGORK/AS; 130 (UP RT), Somchai Som/SS; 131 (UP), Mario Ruiz/The LIFE Images Collection via GI/GI; 131 (LO), Andrea Izzotti/AS; 132 (LE), Allen.G/AS; 132 (RT), snyGGG/AS; 133, antpkr/SS; 134 (UP), Zen Rial/GI; 134 (LO), Alan Welner/AP/SS; 135, SeanPavone Photo/AS; 136 (LE), jubrancoelho/GI; 136 (UP RT), Stuart Monk/AS; 136 (LO RT), Roman Tiraspolsky/AS; 137, Mayumi Nashida/SS; 138, Disney+/Kobal/SS; 139, SeanPavonePhoto/AS; 139 (LO RT), Airin.dizain/ SS; 140, fergregory/AS; 140 (LO LE), Alexander Limbach/SS; 140 (LO CTR), photoDISC/GI; 141 (LE), BullRun/AS; 141 (UP RT), T.Sumaetho/SS; 141 (LO RT), mandritoiu/AS; 142 (UP), Likanaris/AS; 142 (LO), vichie81/AS; 143, Carlo Allegri/Reuters/AS; 144-145, Francois Roux/SS; 146 (LE), Laurentiu Garofeanu/Barcroft USA/Barcoft Media via GI; 146 (UP RT), Stephen Morrison/EPA/SS; 146 (LO RT), photoDISC; 147 (UP), Johannes Schmitt-Tegge/picture alliance via GI; 147 (CTR), John_Dakapu/SS; 147 (LO), Elnur/SS; 148-49, Bettmann/GI; 150 (UP LE), smiltena/AS; 150 (UP RT), Joe Dziemianowicz/NY Daily News Archive via GI; 150 (LO LE), akova/GI; 150 (LO RT), ronstik/AS; 151, Xhibition; 152 (UP LE), Curtis Means/ACE Pictures/SS; 152 (LO LE), Tischenko Irina/SS; 152 (LO RT), vladwel/SS; 153, Barbara C/AS; 154, quietbits/SS; 156, Atlas/AS; 157 (LE), spinetta/AS; 157 (UP CTR), Art_girl/SS; 157 (UP RT), Chanawat/AS; 157 (LO CTR), canbedone/AS; 157 (LO RT), arosoft/SS; 158-159, Felix Lipov/SS; 160 (UP), Laurinson Crusoe/SS; 160 (LO), jordi2r/AS; 161, Ira Berger/Alamy Stock Photo; 162 (LE), Nuttanun/AS; 162 (RT), Lucocattani/AS; 162 (background), francisblack/iStockphoto; 163, Innavector/AS; 164-165, Timothy White/20th Century Fox/Kobal/SS; 165 (LE), Senohrabek/SS; 165 (RT), Marina Monroe/AS; 166 (INSET), Carl.Salisbury/SS; 166, Gordon Donovan/SS; 167 (LE), Stephen Lovekin/BEI/SS; 167 (RT), Will Howe/AS; 168 (UP), Awana JF/SS; 168 (CTR), Everett Collection/SS; 168 (LO), Michael Burrell/GI; 169, Eric Isselée/SS; 170-171, Justin Gignac; 172 (UP), Paul Carluccio; 172 (CTR), Julie Boro/SS; 172 (LO), Annette Shaff/SS; 173 (foreground), Marques/SS; 173 (background), MatViv23/SS; 174 (LE), The Cloisters Collection, 1935/Metropolitan Museum of Art; 174 (UP LE), Alexander Limbach/SS; 174 (UP CTR LE), annbozhko/AS; 174 (UP CTR RT), David Sandonato/Dreamstime; 174 (UP RT), studiovin/SS; 174 (LO RT), lev radin/SS; 175, Yevheniia/AS; 176 (LE), Steven Ferdman/SS; 176 (CTR), Olga Popova/SS; 176 (RT), PhilipYb Studio/SS; 177 (UP LE), Ratana21/SS; 177 (LO LE), Suzumi Abe/thisplate.nyc; 177 (RT), snjadesign/AS; 178 (UP), dlyastokiv/AS; 178 (CTR), Amr Alfiky/Reuters/AS; 178 (LO), lesart777/AS; 179 (UP LE), luplupme/GI; 179 (LO LE), Roman Babakin/AS; 179 (UP RT), Photocreo Bednarek/AS; 179 (LO RT), Yekatseryna/AS; 180-181, Terese Loeb Kreuzer/Alamy Stock Photo; 182, Featureflash Photo Agency/ SS; 183 (UP LE), Mariusz Blach/AS; 183 (LO LE), Porcupen/AS; 183 (RT), Marco Rubino/SS; 184 (LE), USO/ GI; 184 (UP RT), pamela_d_mcadams/AS; 184 (LO RT), Everett Collection/SS; 185 (UP LE), Mary Altaffer/ AP/SS; 185 (UP RT), UI/SS; 185 (LO), Ezra Shaw/GI; 186, 360b/SS; 187 (UP), 5 second Studio/SS; 187 (CTR), Anton Gorbachev/Dreamstime; 187 (LO), kmiragaya/AS; 188 (UP LE), Robert Wilson/AS; 188 (UP RT), grgroup/AS; 188 (LO), Thomas Pajot/AS; 188 (LO LE), Madlen/SS; 188 (LO CTR), Best_photo_ studio/SS; 188 (LO RT), Jiri Miklo/SS; 189, Kathy Willens/AP/SS; 189 (CTR), robertsre/SS; 190, Robert L Kothenbeutel/SS; 191 (UP LE), Jakub Grygier/SS; 191 (LO LE), art_of_sun/SS; 191 (RT), David Brabyn/ Alamy Stock Photo; 192 (UP), Michael Urmann/SS; 192 (LO), mark_ka/AS; 192, PhilipYb Studio/SS; 193 (LE), Rasulov/AS; 193 (RT), Rasulov/AS; 194 (UP), juliars/AS; 194 (CTR), quiggyt4/SS; 194 (LO LE), Pirita/ Dreamstime; 194 (LO RT), Taufik Ramadhan/AS; 195 (UP), TTstudio/AS; 195 (LO LE), gary718/SS; 195 (LO RT), Ignat Zaytsev/SS; 196 (UP), SunnyS/AS; 196 (LO), NASA/Paul E. Alers; 197, a katz/SS

IT DOESN'T END HERE!

Turns out, the whole world is weird! Check out wacky facts about every state in the U.S.A. And New York's neighbor to the north can be pretty wacky, too.

More than 35 Weird But True books!

COLLECT THEM ALL!

NATIONAL GEOGRAPHIC KiDS

AVAILABLE WHEREVER BOOKS ARE SOLD

Discover more at natgeokids.com/wbtbooks

© 2021 National Geographic Partners, LLC